Public Finance and regulation of the Financial System

Shahzoda Norkulova

Public Finance and regulation of the Financial System

By: Shahzoda Norkulova

Edition: June '2025

Publisher:

Taemeer Publications LLC (Michigan, USA / Hyderabad, India)

ISBN 978-93-6908-627-6

9 789369 086276

Book	:	Public Finance and regulation of the Financial System
Author/s	:	Shahzoda Norkulova
Publisher	:	Taemeer Publications
Year	:	'2025
Pages	:	100
Title Design	:	*Taemeer Web Design*

PUBLIC FINANCE AND REGULATION OF THE FINANCIAL SYSTEM

(Collection of articles)

Author:
Sh.I.Norkulova

Scientific adviser:
U.T.To`lakov

ISSUES OF STATE REGULATION OF THE FINANCIAL MARKET

Abstract: This article analyzes the theoretical foundations of state regulation of the financial market, international best practices, and the current situation in the context of the Republic of Uzbekistan. The role of the financial market in the economy, forms of regulation, and the functions of state institutions are explored. Additionally, existing problems in Uzbekistan's financial market are identified, and proposals and recommendations for their resolution are developed. The research applies a scientific approach based on the analysis of data from international organizations, statistical indicators, and normative-legal documents.

Keywords: financial market, state regulation, oversight, stock market, capital market, Central Bank, financial stability, investor rights, economic security, Uzbekistan.

Introduction

The regulation of financial markets holds a significant place in economic theory. Classical economists such as Adam Smith and David Ricardo believed in the self-regulating nature of markets, advocating for minimal state intervention. They argued that market forces naturally determine prices and allocate resources efficiently. However, the economic crises of the early 20th century, particularly the Great Depression of 1929–1933, highlighted the necessity for active state involvement in the economy. John Maynard Keynes emphasized that the state should play a crucial role in ensuring market equilibrium, preventing financial crises, and promoting stable growth. This Keynesian approach led to the emergence of the state as an active regulator in the financial sector.

Modern economic theories, including institutionalism (D. North, O. Williamson), view the efficiency of the state and institutions as essential for the effective functioning of financial markets. Regulatory economics examines financial regulation and its impact on economic efficiency, suggesting that excessive regulation stifles innovation, while insufficient regulation leads to financial instability. Therefore, a balanced regulatory approach is necessary.

Forms of Financial Market Regulation

International practices identify several forms of financial market regulation:

- **Prudential Regulation**: Measures aimed at maintaining financial stability, such as capital adequacy and risk management requirements.

- **Normative Regulation**: Standards governing the conduct of market participants.
- **Market Coordination and Supervision**: Monitoring the activities of financial institutions.
- **Licensing and Accreditation**: Ensuring the legal operation of financial organizations.

In recent years, new directions have emerged in regulatory systems, including macroprudential approaches, digital finance, and the regulation of cryptocurrency markets. International financial institutions such as the IMF, BIS, IOSCO, and the World Bank are developing global standards for effective financial market regulation.

State Regulation of Financial Markets in Uzbekistan

In Uzbekistan, the development of the

financial market is a priority for economic growth, increasing GDP, attracting capital, and enhancing investment attractiveness. President Sh. Mirziyoyev's Decree No. PF-4947 emphasizes the development of the financial market as an alternative source for mobilizing capital and investing free funds of enterprises, financial institutions, and the population. The Decree outlines the concept for the medium- and long-term development of Uzbekistan's financial market. researchgate.net

In a market economy, two approaches to regulating financial market participants have evolved: state regulation and market-based regulation. Market-based regulation relies on the laws of value and supply-demand, ensuring international financial flows in a competitive environment. However, financial markets are influenced by various subjective factors such as political, social, informational, and cultural elements, and may not always be self-regulating. In such cases, state intervention is required. State and market-based regulation complement each other.

Methodology

The regulation and supervision of financial market relations are increasingly important in developing Asian economies, as foreign financial companies expand their participation in regional markets, and regional financial companies broaden their external operations. The growth of financial ties among Asian countries leads to an increase in cross-border financial transactions. Key factors necessitating effective regulation include:

1. Capital inflows from developed economies.
2. Growing international exposure of Asian banks.researchgate.net
3. Demand for foreign investments by Asian households.

4. The role of institutional investors.

Institutional investors in the Asian region, including pension funds, serve as significant channels for the outflow of both private and public funds abroad. Sovereign wealth funds managing national currency reserves may seek foreign investments when foreign assets are relatively undervalued, a trend that may persist even after global financial markets stabilize.

Conclusion

The state budget system in modern economies is not only a tool for financial management but also a crucial mechanism for ensuring economic growth, social equity, infrastructure development, and sustainable development. Through the state budget, various sectors of the national economy are financially supported, social protection is enhanced, and macroeconomic balance is maintained. The composition of budget revenues and their formation mechanisms are vital for ensuring economic stability. Taxes, other mandatory payments, and revenues from state assets are the primary sources of the state budget, and their mismanagement can lead to economic imbalances. A well-structured, efficient, and transparent budget system positively impacts a country's economic sovereignty, fiscal stability, and investment attractiveness.

Financial markets play a crucial role in ensuring the stable and consistent development of the economy. Effective regulation enhances macroeconomic balance, investment activity, and financial confidence. While positive results have been achieved in regulating Uzbekistan's financial market, challenges remain, such as inconsistent legal documents, a limited number of market participants, and low information transparency for investors. Future improvements should focus on digitization, strengthening institutional capacity, and aligning with international standards.

References

1. **Mirziyoyev, Sh.** (2017). *Decree No. PF-4947 of the President of the Republic of Uzbekistan "On the Strategy of Actions for Further Development of the Republic of Uzbekistan"*. February 17, 2017. Retrieved from: https://lex.uz/docs/-3107036
2. **Keynes, J.M.** (1936). *The General Theory of Employment, Interest and Money*. Macmillan.
3. **Amadeo, K.** (2020). *Financial Regulations*. The Balance, March 14. Retrieved from: https://www.thebalance.com/financial-regulations-3306234
4. **Ataniyazov, J., & Alimardonov, E.** (2014). *International Financial Relations*. Textbook. Tashkent: Uzbekistan Philosophers' National Society Publishing.

Retrieved from: http://el.tfi.uz/images/Xalqaro_moliya_munosabatlari_a4e0e.pdf

5. **Kawai, M., & Prasad, E.S.** (2011). *Financial Market Regulation and Reforms in Emerging Markets.* Asian Development Bank Institute & The Brookings Institution. Retrieved from: https://www.adb.org/sites/default/files/publication/159338/adbifinancialmarketregulationand-reforms-emerging-markets-highlights.pdf
6. **International Monetary Fund (IMF).** (2023). *Global Financial Stability Report.*
7. **International Organization of Securities Commissions (IOSCO).** (2017). *Objectives and Principles of Securities Regulation.*
8. **Islomov, B., & Khodjayev, S.** (2020). *"Uzbekistan's Financial Market:*

Development Status and Prospects." Economics and Innovative Technologies, No. 5.

9. **Khudoyqulova, N.** (2021). *"Legal Foundations of Financial Market Regulation."* Scientific Bulletin of Tashkent State University of Economics, No. 2.

THE STATE BUDGET SYSTEM AND THE FORMATION OF REVENUES

Abstract: This article analyzes the structure of the state budget system and its main functions, the sources of budget revenue formation, and their role in ensuring economic stability. Particular attention is given to the formation of budget revenues in the Republic of Uzbekistan, the share of taxes and other mandatory payments, the effectiveness of fiscal policy, and directions for its improvement. The study employs an analytical approach based on existing legislation, statistical data, and advanced international practices.

Keywords: state budget, budget system, budget revenues, fiscal policy, taxes

Introduction

The state budget is one of the key financial

instruments in a country's economic system, playing a crucial role in managing socio-economic development, financing government expenditures, and ensuring macroeconomic stability. Through the budget system, financial resources are redistributed at both the central and local levels. The targeted and efficient use of these resources has a direct impact on the success of government policies.

In recent years, the Republic of Uzbekistan has implemented several practical measures to reform its budget policy, enhance transparency, and expand its revenue base. Notably, significant achievements have been made in digitizing budget processes, simplifying tax administration, and ensuring transparency.

The main objective of this article is to identify the factors influencing the state budget system and the formation of its revenues, analyze existing problems, and develop recommendations for their solution. For this purpose, the research is based on national and international experiences, statistical data, and normative-legal documents.

Research Methodology

A comprehensive methodological approach was used to deeply analyze the budget system and the formation of budget revenues. The research employed theoretical, statistical, and empirical methods. The main applied methods include:

1. **Theoretical analysis** – Used to explore the nature, functions, historical development, and modern role of the state budget in economic management, based on economic theories and legal documents. It covered:
    - Structure and principles of the budget system
    - Classification of budget revenues
    - Types of fiscal policy and their impact on the economy
2. **Statistical analysis** – Based on data from

the Ministry of Finance, the State Tax Committee, the State Statistics Committee of Uzbekistan, and the World Bank (2020–2024), covering:

- Dynamics of state budget revenues
- Structure of taxes and other revenues
- Distribution between central and local budgets

3. **Comparative analysis** – By comparing Uzbekistan's budget system and revenue formation with countries like Poland, Malaysia, and Estonia, the study identified:
   - Best practices for ensuring budget stability
   - Strengths and weaknesses of Uzbekistan's experience
4. **Empirical analysis** – Examining the practical effects of laws, regulatory documents, and reform programs, focusing on:

- Impact of tax incentives on budget revenues
- Effects of digital technologies on tax collection

5. **Expert opinion and content analysis** – Opinions of experts, economists, and practitioners were reviewed through interviews and publications. Legislative documents were also analyzed to assess the direction of budget policy.

Analysis and Results

1. **Structure of Budget revenues (2020–2024)**

Source	**2020** (%)	**2021** (%)	**2022** (%)	**2023** (%)	**2024** (%)
Taxes	60	62	64	65	66
Other mandatory payments	20	18	17	16	15

Source	2020 (%)	2021 (%)	2022 (%)	2023 (%)	2024 (%)
Revenues from state assets	10	12	11	10	9
Other sources	10	8	8	9	10

2. **Ratio of Budget Revenues to GDP (2020–2024):**

Year	Budget Revenues (bln UZS)	GDP (bln UZS)	Revenue-to-GDP (%)
2020	100,000	500,000	20
2021	110,000	550,000	20
2022	120,000	600,000	20
2023	130,000	650,000	20
2024	140,000	700,000	20

The analysis results indicate that from 2020 to 2024, the main share of the state budget revenues of the Republic of Uzbekistan

was formed by taxes. Specifically, in 2020, 60% of total revenues came from taxes, and by 2024 this figure had increased to 66%. This reflects a steady year-on-year growth in tax revenues and highlights their growing importance in maintaining fiscal stability.

At the same time, the share of other mandatory payments has shown a declining trend. While these accounted for 20% of revenues in 2020, their share dropped to 15% by 2024. This suggests either a reduction in certain payments or a relative decline in their significance compared to taxes.

Revenues from state property and assets have shown a steady downward trend: while this figure was 10% in 2020, it declined to 9% by 2024. This situation indicates the need to improve the efficiency of utilizing state assets.

Another important indicator is the ratio of budget revenues to gross domestic product

(GDP). From 2020 to 2024, this figure remained stable at around 20% annually. This indicates that the state budget revenues are growing proportionally to the size of the national economy, and fiscal stability is being maintained. Overall, these figures demonstrate the dominance of a tax-based budget policy in Uzbekistan. However, the relative decline of other income sources also underscores the need for fiscal diversification.

CONCLUSION

The research results show that the state budget system is not only a financial management tool in a modern economy but also an essential mechanism for ensuring economic growth, social equity, infrastructure development, and sustainable progress. Through the state budget, various sectors of the national economy receive financial support, the social protection of the population is strengthened, and macroeconomic balance is maintained.

The composition of budget revenues and the mechanisms of their formation play a critical role in ensuring economic stability. Taxes, other mandatory payments, and revenues from state property constitute the main sources of the state budget. If not managed effectively, these sources can lead to economic imbalances.

The analysis based on statistics from 2020–2024 shows that tax revenues dominate within total income, and their share has increased year by year. This confirms the prioritization of a tax-based fiscal policy. In addition, the stable ratio of budget revenues to GDP at around 20% reflects balanced fiscal management by the state. However, the declining share of other income sources, particularly from state assets and mandatory payments, highlights the necessity of diversifying state revenue streams.

In general, if the state budget system and revenue

formation processes are managed in a systematic, efficient, and transparent manner, this will positively influence the country's economic sovereignty, fiscal stability, and investment attractiveness.

References:

1. Budget Code of the Republic of Uzbekistan. – Tashkent: Adolat, 2023.
2. Decrees and decisions of the President of the Republic of Uzbekistan (on budget policy in recent years).
3. Main directions of tax and budget policy. Reports of the Ministry of Finance of the Republic of Uzbekistan (2022–2024).
4. Musayev B. Sh., Rakhmonqulov A. *Economic Theory*. – Tashkent: IQTISOD-MOLIYA, 2021.
5. Tanzi V., Schuknecht L. *Public Spending in the 20th Century: A Global Perspective*.

Cambridge University Press, 2000.

6. IMF Fiscal Monitor Reports. International Monetary Fund, www.imf.org
7. World Bank. *Public Finance Reviews for Uzbekistan*. www.worldbank.org
8. Karimov I.A. *Uzbekistan – On the Path to Market Relations*. – Tashkent: Uzbekistan, 1994.
9. Qosimov D., Yusupov M. *Public Finance*. – Tashkent: Iqtisodiyot, 2022.
10. OECD. *Revenue Statistics Database*. www.oecd.org

THE CONCEPT OF FINANCE AND ITS FUNCTIONS

Annotation: This article provides comprehensive coverage of the concept of finance, the importance of finance, the functions performed by finance, the resource of Finance i.e. financial target monetary funds, the object of which is calculated, and the interrelationships of financial functions, complementing one.

Keywords: Finance, functions of Finance, trans-ferts payments, targeted monetary funds, Gross Domestic Product (GDP), tax, state budget, financing, economy.

Finance is the aggregate of economic relations arising from the formation, accumulation, distribution, redistribution, or use of centralized and decentralized targeted monetary funds. Finance is a category that arises in the monetary sector of the economy, based on income.

Through the movement of money and money-equivalent assets, monetary funds are created that form the state budget. When we talk about targeted monetary funds, we refer to financial resources or financial objects. Alongside the financial object, the financial subject can be defined as the participants involved in creating, distributing, and using these funds — including enterprises (firms), various economic units, households, non-governmental public organizations, and government institutions.

Finance means generating income and spending it. Furthermore, the financial system plays a major role in the creation and preservation of the state budget because finance generates income and ensures the circulation of monetary funds through expenditure.

Initially, through primary distribution of income, enterprise, state, and household finances emerge, resulting in primary incomes. Enterprises form financial funds; workers receive their wages, which primarily drives household income. A portion of state income arises when enterprises pay taxes to the budget. When incomes are redistributed secondarily, transfers (payments) from the budget and various special funds are allocated. Upon further redistribution, various non-governmental and public organizations receive funds from enterprises, organizations, the population, and the budget to form their special funds.

Finance performs five important functions in the economy as monetary relations:

1. **Distribution (Allocation) Function**
2. **Development Function**
3. **Social Protection Function**
4. **Information Function**
5. **Control Functio**

Distribution (Allocation) Function of Finance

The essence of this function is that in the first stage of the distribution process of the gross domestic (national) product (national income) created by society in the production sector, it is distributed among its creators in various forms (income, profit, interest, dividends, rent, lease, wages, bonuses, etc.). Then, at the secondary distribution stage, national income is redistributed through taxes, resulting in a permanent allocation of funds within various monetary funds of different levels. If we focus on the distribution process, finance participates in the third stage of distribution.

Development Function of Finance

The development of finance and stimulating the activity of economic entities is of great importance. Incentives are implemented through financial instruments such as rewards, subsidies, subventions, fines, sanctions, and taxation. In a tax market, taxation is the main incentive tool. Various tax incentives increase the income of taxpayers and encourage them to work better.

Social Protection Function of Finance

Disadvantaged or needy populations receive financial assistance from the state, enterprises, various non-governmental organizations, and wealthy citizens. To fulfill this task, the state budget allocates funds specifically for social protection.

Information Function of Finance

This function provides information about the financial condition of the country and individual entities. Through these indicators, the state can find solutions to problems hindering economic development.

Control Function of Finance

This function involves monitoring whether funds in various monetary funds are spent purposefully, efficiently, and targeted. It is important to note that this function is mainly performed by authorized state bodies. The existence and functioning of finance are linked to state activities. Finance is a continuous process of control through state activities. For this reason, many economists emphasize the importance of this function.

When discussing the functions of finance, it is necessary to consider their stability and variability, as it helps understand the differences between them. The distribution function of finance is permanent, and based on its content, the level of other functions is determined. For example, if the control function weakens, it may lead to the improper distribution of monetary funds since financial control reveals whether funds are used efficiently or inefficiently.

In general, it can be concluded that the functions

of finance are interconnected and complement each other. Their practical activities are always influenced by the state's financial policy.

References:

1. Elmirzayev S. *Corporate Finance*. Textbook. Uzbek State University of World Languages and Uzbek-Turkish Madrasa Institute. – Tashkent: "Iqtisod-moliya", 2015.
2. Richard A. Brealey, Stewart C. Myers, Franklin Allen. *Fundamentals of Corporate Finance*. Seventh Global Edition.– McGraw-Hill Education, 2014.
3. Khudoyqulov Sadirdin Karimovich. *Finance and Taxes*. Textbook. Tashkent – 2020.
4. National Encyclopedia of Uzbekistan (2000–2005). Uzbek National Encyclopedia. Volume One. Tashkent,

2020.

5. https://uz.wikipedia.org/wiki/Moliya.
National Encyclopedia of Uzbekistan (2000–2005).

SOURCES OF STATE BUDGET INCOME AND PROCEDURE FOR THEIR FORMATION

Abstract: This article describes in detail the sources of the state budget and state budget revenues, which are of great importance in the formation and development of state finances. In addition, it was discussed in detail that the effective disposal of the state budget affects not only the macroeconomic development of the country, but also the economy of economic entities.

Key words: State budget, financing, various taxes collected from the population, receipts from signature bonus and commercial discovery bonus, dividends, Central Bank, local budget revenues.

To timely and fully resolve the socio-economic tasks of the state, a certain financial basis must exist. At the core of this financial foundation lies the **state budget**. The key process in forming any budget is identifying its sources of revenue. It is important to emphasize that in most countries worldwide, the main source of state budget revenues is taxes and other mandatory payments, and these revenue sources are defined by law.

Currently, in the Republic of Uzbekistan, reforms aimed at improving and developing state finance within the budget system, ensuring the stability of state budget revenues, and perfecting the completeness and sources of their formation have gained crucial importance.

Efficient organization of financial relations within the state budget system ultimately contributes to the successful execution of the budget. If the state budget is properly and wisely organized, on one hand, it ensures macroeconomic stability of the country, and on the other, it positively influences the economic activities of business entities, leading to the economic development of the country. This, in turn, plays an important role in the stability of the country's financial system. Therefore, improving the mechanism of forming state budget revenues and ensuring the stability of budget revenues remain pressing issues.

Sources of State Budget Revenues of the Republic of Uzbekistan

The sources of the state budget revenues are clearly defined in the Budget Code of the Republic of Uzbekistan and include the following:

- Taxes and other mandatory payments;
- Revenues from placement, use, and sale of state assets;
- Monetary funds transferred to state property by inheritance or gift rights;

- Non-repayable cash receipts from legal and natural persons, as well as from foreign states;
- Payments from the repayment of budget loans to resident legal persons and credits allocated to foreign states;
- Other revenues in accordance with legal acts.

Sources of the Republican Budget Revenues of Uzbekistan

The sources of the republican budget revenues include:

1. **General state taxes**, including:
    - Profit tax from legal entities;
    - Single tax payment;
    - Income tax from individuals;
    - Value-added tax (VAT);
    - Excise tax;
    - Land use tax.
2. **Customs duties**;

3. **Additional profit tax**;
4. **State share of profit from product distribution agreements**;
5. **Other revenues**, such as:
   - Income from signed bonuses and commercial finders' fees;
   - State duties, fees, compensation payments, fines and sanctions directed to the republican budget in accordance with the law;
   - Revenues from placement, use, and sale of state assets based on established norms;
   - Monetary funds transferred to state property by inheritance or gift rights;
   - Non-repayable cash receipts from legal and natural persons, as well as from foreign states;
   - Payments from repayment of budget loans to resident legal persons and

credits allocated to foreign states;

- Dividends from the state share in stocks;
- Payments for the use of subscriber numbers by legal entities providing mobile communication services;
- Profits of the Central Bank of Uzbekistan;
- Other revenues stipulated by legislation.

In summary, the essence of the state budget of any country is connected to its centralized monetary fund. The state budget, as a form of centralized monetary funds and as part of the budget system, holds significant importance in the financial mechanism of any state.

References

1. Khudoyqulov Sadirdin Karimovich. *Finance and Taxes*. Textbook. Tashkent –

2020.
2. https://api.ziyonet.uz/uploads/books/835095/5d08d6d1acda4.pdf (Tursunmurodova, 2023).
3. “Definition of Taxes”. OECD (April 19, 1996). Accessed March 23, 2022.
4. Budget Code of the Republic of Uzbekistan. Law No. O'RQ-360, December 26, 2013. Collection of Legal Acts of the Republic of Uzbekistan.
5. Law No. O'RQ-589, December 9, 2019, "On the State Budget of the Republic of Uzbekistan for 2020."

TAX SYSTEM AND ITS TYPES ACCORDING TO THE TAX OBJECT

Abstract: In this article, there is detailed information about the tax system and its specific types, which are considered to be the process of mutually complementing the elements that reflect all the relations related to the application of taxes in society. information is provided. In addition, when talking about the tax system, it is permissible to mention that the difference between the concepts of the tax system and the taxation system has been explained in detail.

Key words: Tax, concept of system, economy, taxes on turnover, income and property value, taxation system, Supreme Assembly, taxpayers, state, market economy.

Any relationships operating in the economy function in the form of a **system**. A system is understood as the implementation of interconnected and complementary internal elements. The main condition for a system is that it must have two or more elements that interact with each other to ensure the functioning of the system. Therefore, the system exists not only as a broad category and relationship but also each of its elements functions as a system itself. In other words, a system is considered as an aggregate until it encompasses smaller elements.

For example, the **tax system** includes elements such as tax policy strategy, tactics, and concept. Tax policy itself and each of its elements exist as systems. The strategy, as an element of tax policy, consists of components like development, implementation, and improvement. Studying any process as a system helps first to understand the essence of that system, and second, to identify the degree of interconnection of its aspects.

Thus, the concept of a system serves as a unifying category for describing relationships and brings together all elements that belong to the system.

Definition and Classification of the Tax System

Simply put, the **tax system** refers to the aggregate of tax types that are homogeneous in essence and contribute to the centralized monetary fund.

The tax system can be divided into the following groups based on the tax base:

- Taxes on turnover value;
- Taxes on income value;
- Taxes on property value.

Taxes on turnover include value-added tax (VAT), excise tax, tax for using mineral resources, and customs duties. Taxes on income include profit tax and income tax. Taxes on property include property tax and land tax.

Distinction Between Tax System and

Taxation System

It is essential to distinguish between the concepts of **tax system** and **taxation system**. The tax system theoretically refers to the aggregate of taxes. The taxation system, however, refers organizationally to the aggregate of structural methods of tax collection. In other words, the taxation system is a set of practical methods.

The taxation system forms a part of the tax system but has a narrower meaning. While the tax system covers all relationships related to taxes, the taxation system includes economic and legal relationships concerning tax collection.

From this perspective, the taxation system is a set of methods, elements, and principles established by legislative power through law and implemented by executive authorities for tax collection.

Thus, based on legal norms and executed by authorities, the aggregate of methods, elements, and principles for structuring and collecting taxes is called the **taxation system**.

In conclusion, the tax system is the totality of taxes collected for the benefit of the state under certain conditions, including the organization of methods and means of tax collection. Taxes are inseparable from the existence of the state. The tax system plays a significant role in the development of the country's economy. To date, no other method besides taxes has been globally used to generate financial resources necessary for the state's functions. Therefore, as long as the state exists as a ruling power, taxes remain the primary method of financing

REFERENCES

1. https://vaqt.ucoz.com/publ/iqtisod_va_moliya/o_zbekistonda_soliq_byudjet_siyosati_va_soliq_tizimining_xususiyatlari/28-1-0-278
2. Khudoyqulov Sadirdin Karimovich.

Finance and Taxes. Textbook. Tashkent – 2020.

3. Elbayeva Muqaddas Rashidovna. *Improvement of Tax Risk Management in the Tax System*. PhD Dissertation Abstract. Tashkent – 2023.
4. A. V. Vahobov, A. S. Jo'rayev. *Taxes and Taxation*. Recommended textbook by the Ministry of Higher and Secondary Specialized Education of Uzbekistan. «Sharq» Publishing House, Tashkent — 2009.
5. Tax Code of the Republic of Uzbekistan, December 30, 2019.
6. Ministry of Higher and Secondary Specialized Education of Uzbekistan, Mirzo Ulugbek National University, Faculty of Economics. *Finance and Taxes* Lecture Course. Tashkent – 2012.

FINANCIAL POLICY AND ITS STRUCTURE

Abstract: This article describes in detail the financial policy, which is the independent activity of the state in the field of financial relations aimed at providing appropriate financial resources for the implementation of one or another economic and social development program of the state, as well as its structural structure, which allows a full understanding of the financial policy.

Key words: Financial management, budget transfers, credit, state, budget revenues, family business, household, non-profit organizations, financial resources, money funds, financial quotas, profit, bank deposits, savings, society, interest rates.

As long as the state carries out its activities, it implements various policies. The entire financial management system operates based on the state's **financial policy**. Therefore, it is no exaggeration to say that financial policy is the most important element of the financial management system. Financial policy functions across all sectors. Even the family, considered the basic unit of society, participates in economic relations as an economic lifestyle or in the form of a family business, managing the family budget or family business budget. Naturally, within its own scope, the family possesses its own financial policy. Hence, financial policy is applied in almost all activities.

Financial policy can independently implement state policy in any area of social activity. It is important to first understand its structural composition to better grasp financial policy. Based on its scope, financial policy is classified as follows:

- **State-level financial policy**

- **Financial policy of economic entities**
- **Financial policy of non-profit organizations**
- **Financial policy of households**

State-Level Financial Policy

State-level financial policy reflects the process of forming and utilizing financial resources and funds at various levels necessary for the state to fulfill its socio-economic functions. It includes measures aimed at regulating the economy and ensuring an average standard of living in households through financial instruments such as financial quotas, interest rates, budget transfers, and financial requirements imposed on organizations.

The core activities of state financial policy include:

- Formation of centralized monetary funds;
- Identification of income sources;
- Attracting revenues into centralized

monetary funds and allocating them according to planned budgets;

- Application of financial instruments to develop and regulate the national economy;
- Conducting scientific and theoretical processes aimed at determining directions for financial management.

Financial Policy of Economic Entities and Non-Profit Organizations

The financial policy of economic entities is determined by their legal-organizational form, regulations, and financial laws. If an entity's legal structure and statutes specify non-profit activities, it adopts a specific financial policy; if profit-making, the financial policy corresponds accordingly.

Therefore, financial policy in this context can be divided into:

- **Profit-oriented financial policy**
- **Activity-supporting financial policy**

The profit-oriented policy is self-explanatory. The activity-supporting financial policy, on the other hand, involves non-profit organizations (according to their statutes, they are not aimed at profit-making) that identify financial resource needs for a certain period, develop spending plans, ensure targeted and efficient use of resources, generate additional income through entrepreneurial activity without violating laws, and invest surplus funds in bank deposits to earn interest.

Financial Policy of Households

Households represent both a social unit and an economic agent consuming goods and services or acting as a business entity in the form of a family business. Thus, families manage incomes, expenses, savings, and debts (for example, taking loans from credit institutions to start a business).

In summary, the state uses finance to fulfill its functions and goals in any society. Financial policy plays a crucial role in achieving these objectives. It provides financial resources for implementing state plans and measures for social and economic development. Additionally, financial policy, while being independent, serves as an essential tool for the state to carry out any desired activity—whether social, economic, or international relations.

References:

1. Uzbekistan National Encyclopedia (2000-2005). First Volume. Tashkent, 2000.
2. Khudoyqulov Sadirdin Karimovich. *Finance and Taxes*. Textbook. Tashkent – 2020.
3. Yoldoshev Z., Malikov T. *Household Finance*. Textbook. Tashkent, "IQTISOD-MOLIYA," 2008.
4. Ministry of Higher and Secondary Specialized Education of Uzbekistan,

Mirzo Ulugbek National University, Faculty of Economics. *Finance and Taxes* Lecture Course. Tashkent – 2012.

5. Vahobov A. et al. *Financial and Managerial Analysis*. Textbook. Tashkent, Sharq, 2005.
6. https://prezi.com/p/eiwbaubqsilc/moliyaviy-siyosat/

INFORMATION TECHNOLOGIES IN THE ECONOMY AND WAYS TO USE THEIR SYSTEMS

Abstract: The importance of automation of business processes in the modern economy is considered in detail in the article. Automation is presented as an indispensable tool that allows enterprises to increase operational efficiency, reduce errors, and save time and resources. The advantages of automation will be emphasized, as well as the problems and difficulties that may arise during its implementation.

Keywords: Automation, business processes, digital transformation, efficiency, innovation, national income, commodity, e-commerce, e-business, virtual commerce, virtual education, distance learning, virtual stand technologies.

Information systems and technologies are increasingly being applied in various spheres of human activity year by year. The purpose of creating, implementing, and widely applying them is to solve problems related to informatization of society and human life activities. Informatization of society means the comprehensive measures aimed at ensuring the full and timely use of enriched knowledge and reliable information in all socially significant fields of human activity.

This implies that the application of modern information systems and technologies everywhere increases the effectiveness of decisions to be made. This not only promotes economic growth indicators of national development but also ensures scientific achievements in fundamental and applied sciences aimed at developing production, creating new jobs, improving living standards, and protecting the environment.

In the new 21st century, the national economy of countries is becoming globalized and transforming into an information-based economy. The role of information and knowledge in the national economy is steadily increasing, turning them into strategic resources. It is notable that 90% of the world's accumulated information and knowledge has been created in the last 30 years. The growing volume of information and knowledge requires extensive and effective use of information and communication technologies (ICT) in all sectors, including education.

Information has become a resource that, like traditional resources, can be searched for and distributed. The total volume of this resource in use will determine the strategic potential of states in the future, as well as their defense capabilities.

Efficient organization and use of information resources reveal that they are equivalent to labor, material, and energy resources. At the same time, information is the only resource that helps in the rational and effective use of all other resources and their preservation.

Thus, information resources in a modern information society are not only a major part of production but also a commodity serving as a source of national income.

Information technologies function both as independent systems for data processing and as functional components ensuring management processes within larger systems. Such systems include industrial enterprises, firms, corporations, financial-credit and commercial organizations, automated control of production and economic processes, scientific experiments, economic-mathematical models, data processing systems, library services, and various other sectors.

The global education system is rapidly developing. For example, in the Netherlands, highly qualified graduates are increasingly unemployed. Therefore, it is necessary to carefully study the demand for our specialists. If there is no demand for such personnel in the domestic market, it is necessary to search for external demand through the Internet. It should be emphasized that 85% of professors in U.S. universities are Indians. Their success can be explained by their deep knowledge of exact sciences, excellent foreign language skills, and effective use of information and communication technologies in the national economy and education sectors.

Nowadays, not only in education but also in all branches of the national economy, the Internet, e-commerce, e-business, virtual trade, virtual education, distance learning, and virtual stand technologies are being widely introduced. The penetration of ICT into all spheres of life fundamentally changes the mechanisms of conducting business and education.

It should be noted that in the context of the globalization of the world economy, the labor market size for offering education services via the Internet is limitless. The introduction of ICT in our national economy and ensuring the security of information stored in databases creates new challenges.

Information attacks mean the intentional violation of rules for handling information that can cause significant damage to an enterprise. Often, malicious individuals gain access to computer systems either due to obvious errors or mistakes in implementing protection software.

According to DataPro Research Center, the main causes of damage to electronic information in recent years are distributed as follows: human error – 52%, deliberate actions – 10%, technical failures – 13%, damage due to fire – 15%, and damage due to water – 7-10%. It is clear that in one out of every ten cases, damage to electronic data is related to intentional actions.

What are the consequences of organized attacks on information? First of all, economic damage is of concern:

- Disclosure of commercial information can seriously harm the market situation;
- News of theft of large amounts of information affects a company's reputation and indirectly leads to a decrease in trading volume;
- Competitor firms may use stolen information.

If theft is not detected, the company can be forced into harmful deals leading to its collapse.

Replacing or tampering with information during transmission or storage can cause significant damage to a company. Repeated successful attacks on an information service provider can cause the loss of customer trust, affecting revenue.

Nowadays, computer viruses are among malicious tools used for harmful purposes. According to Panda Software (March 2003), the main viruses causing damage were Klez.I (13.8%), NiceHello (7%), and Enerkaz (6%).

Computer attacks cause not only material but also significant moral damage because users' trust in information decreases, and restoring information to its original state in computer memory becomes very difficult.

The system concept considers the interconnection between its elements. An element without any connection to others is not part of the system.

System properties include complexity, goal orientation, diversity, composition, and division.

In general, a system is not only described differently from its constituent elements qualitatively but also has functions that its elements do not perform individually. A system has a general property, i.e., it strives to achieve a common goal.

In conclusion, modern information technologies are encountered everywhere today. Teaching students to use modern information and pedagogical technologies, and enabling them to use new information technologies and interactive methods in their fields promotes a broader understanding of the studied subject and strengthens knowledge, skills, and competencies. Thus, as the number of users of ICT increases daily, methods of using them continue to improve.

References:

1. https://miastoprzyszlosci.com.pl/index.php/mp/article/view/1966
2. Nurmuxamad Duisenov. Technologies for Processing Economic Information.

3. Abduqodirov A.A., Hayitov A.G., Shodiyev R.R. Information Technologies. Textbook for Academic Lyceums and Vocational Colleges. - Tashkent: “O‘qituvchi”.
4. National Program for Personnel Training // Public Education. 1998. No. 1. P. 5-41.
5. Urishev, B., & Parpiev, G. Using Biometric Methods in Ensuring Information Security.

NATURE AND METHODS OF FINANCIAL MECHANISM

Abstract: This article describes in detail the financial mechanism, which has an important place in the economic category. In addition, detailed information is given on the small mechanisms that make up the composition of the financial mechanism and the methods of the financial mechanism in order for the financial category to be valid within the framework of relations.

Key words: Economic category, national economy, state, price, tax, credit rates, subsidy, economic policy, financial elements, financing, financial resources, methods of financial mechanism.

Every economic category has its own mechanisms. The mechanisms of economic categories depend on the internal essence of the category, its place within economic relations, and the economic system on which the national economy is based. Moreover, there are such economic categories whose mechanisms of operation depend on the activities of the state and socio-economic processes. For example, prices, taxes, subsidies, interest rates, and similar categories are primarily determined by the state's economic policy, which defines their relationships.

The functioning of the financial category does not happen spontaneously; it requires organizational, economic, legal, and normative methods that activate it and ensure its continuous operation. These methods unite with a common purpose to enable the functioning of finance and serve as its mechanisms. From this perspective, the financial mechanism means the set of forms and methods of organizing financial relations, establishing them, forming and distributing financial resources in money funds, as well as the financial elements and instruments applied in financial relations.

Thus, different forms of organizing financial mechanisms can be called financial mechanisms. Centralized monetary funds, which form the material basis for financing state activities, are served by various financial elements; without applying and using these elements, it is impossible to form financial resources. Furthermore, the organizational methods for applying these financial elements are necessary, and financing is carried out using financial instruments. This whole system operates together in the form of financial mechanisms.

If we look at the essence of financial mechanisms from the point of view of their composition, they consist of the following:

Finance mechanism

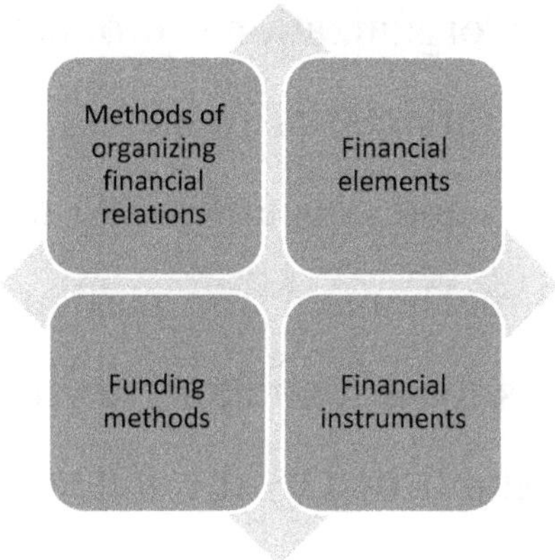

Thus, from a structural point of view, smaller mechanisms that make up the financial mechanism mentioned above are necessary; without them, it is impossible to ensure the full functioning of financial relations. The basis of the financial mechanism is formed by the methods of organizing financial relations.

In conclusion, the financial mechanism is an internal financial management system aimed at establishing effective financial relations and generating funds. If we analyze this system using the example of an enterprise, it affects the final results of the organization's production or other activities and reflects its monetary relations with partner entities and consumers. At the same time, the financial mechanism of a particular enterprise is based on its local regulatory documents as well as the laws established by the state.

References:

1. Enterprise Financial Mechanism and Its Elements | Finance 2024 (periodicalfinance.com). Video. 2024.
2. Khudoyqulov Sadirdin Karimovich. Finance and Taxes. Study Guide. Tashkent – 2020.
3. Vahobov A. et al. Financial and Managerial Analysis. Textbook. T. Sharq, 2005.
4. Financial Policy and Financial Mechanism (arxiv.uz).
5. G'afurov U.V. Main Directions for

Improving the Structural Composition of Small Business in Uzbekistan. "International Finance and Accounting" Scientific Electronic Journal. No. 2, April 2018.

THE IMPORTANCE OF THE STATE BUDGET IN THE DEVELOPMENT OF THE ECONOMY

Abstract: This article provides detailed information about the role of the state budget, which forms the financial basis of the state's economic capabilities as the main financial plan of the state, in the development of the economy, and the main features of the state budget as an economic category.

Key words: State budget, economy, policy, state finance, GDP, national income, income and expenses, taxes, gross budget, gross budget, market economy, budget features, state administration, financing.

In the independent development of every country, pursuing an independent economic policy that aligns with the interests of society is one of the essential conditions. The consistent implementation of such a policy is a decisive factor in ensuring the independence, consolidation, and further development of our country. The foundation of this policy is the implementation of a market economy aimed at satisfying the interests of members of society. The state budget is a category that provides the conditions for implementing such policies of the state.

Today, in the context of liberalization and the free development of our national economy, public finance—and one of its main components, the state budget—plays a particularly important role. Government regulation is crucial in shaping and developing the economic and social structure of society. One of the tools that allows the state to fulfill its functions and implement its economic and social policies is the state budget.

The state budget holds significant

importance in the formation and development of public finance. In the early stages of budget creation, it was common to exaggerate expenditures and revenues; information about taxes and other revenues collected into the budget, as well as the costs associated with their collection, were often not reflected in the budget. To prevent such situations, the gross budget (or "brutto-budget") approach was introduced.

The state budget accumulates a portion of national income and redistributes it across the national economy in various ways. In this process, a larger share is allocated to the non-production sectors, which in turn directly or indirectly impact the production sectors. This function is part of the budget's role in ensuring proportionality between different sectors.

Budgetary relations are an integral part of a society's economic system. Their existence is objectively determined by the need to form a material and financial base necessary for the state to carry out its functions. As a financial foundation of the state's economic capabilities, the state budget is directly linked to the emergence of the state itself. At the same time, in a market economy, the budget becomes a key instrument for carrying out state reforms in the social and economic spheres. The qualitative attributes of the budget are thus clarified.

As an economic category, the budget has the following characteristics:

- **Historical nature** – The budget, as a category, has historically formed and developed with unique characteristics in different states, a trend that continues today.
- **Planning nature** – A key feature of the budget is its planned nature.
- **Legal character** – The budget, as a regulatory document, has the force of law.

- **Time-bound nature** – The budget is prepared and implemented for a specified period.

As an economic category, the state budget represents a system of monetary relations between the state and legal and natural persons regarding the redistribution of gross domestic product and, specifically, the national income—its active part. The result of this process is the creation of a financial fund—the state budget—which is allocated for financing the economy, socio-cultural sectors, defense, and public administration, and is used purposefully.

References:

7. Khudoyqulov Sadirdin Karimovich. *Finance and Taxes*. Study Guide. Tashkent – 2020.
8. J.R. Zaynalov, B.Sh. Xusanov, S.S. Aliyeva, Sh.M. Latipova. *Economics and Finance*. Study Guide. Tashkent – 2021.

9. Ministry of Higher and Secondary Specialized Education of the Republic of Uzbekistan, Mirzo Ulugbek National University of Uzbekistan, Faculty of Economics. *Lecture Course: Finance and Taxes*. Tashkent – 2012.
10. https://uz.wikipedia.org/wiki/Davlat_byudjeti

OPERATIONS OF COMMERCIAL BANKS

Abstract: This article is about commercial banks, which are large credit institutions that provide universal banking services (accounting, payment operations, attraction of deposits, keeping deposits, granting loans, as well as operations on the stock market) to enterprises, organizations, and citizens, and its various operations. explained in detail.

Key words: Passive, capital, liabilities, borrowed funds, deposit, interest, payments, liabilities, authorized fund, income, loan, debt, creditworthiness, solvency, lease, share, bond , factoring, microcredit, deposit, loan.

Despite the global spread of the financial crisis, the banking system of Uzbekistan stands out for its reliability and stable development, as well as its resilience to the negative impacts of external crises.

A commercial bank forms its monetary resources mainly through deposits, interbank loans, and the issuance of its own shares and bonds in order to carry out banking activities.

Bank operations refer to the activities carried out by banks, including accepting money into current or other accounts, issuing loans with or without interest, executing exchange orders, purchasing securities or shares, fulfilling clients' instructions, issuing loans against collateral in the form of goods or commercial documents, and conducting various monetary and non-cash settlement operations.

Throughout 2016, special attention was paid to attracting the idle funds of the population and economic entities to bank deposits by significantly improving the quality of banking services provided to clients, in particular, introducing new types of deposits that matched customer needs.

By the end of 2016, the total volume of deposits attracted by commercial banks increased by 25.2% compared to 2015, reaching 44.6 trillion Uzbek soums.

The second stage in organizing banking activities involves the formation of bank resources. These generated resources are used to support the commercial and economic activities of the banks.

Operations related to the formation of bank resources are known as **passive operations**. Bank resources are formed through these passive operations carried out by banks. Commercial banks use passive operations to establish the credit resources needed for lending purposes.

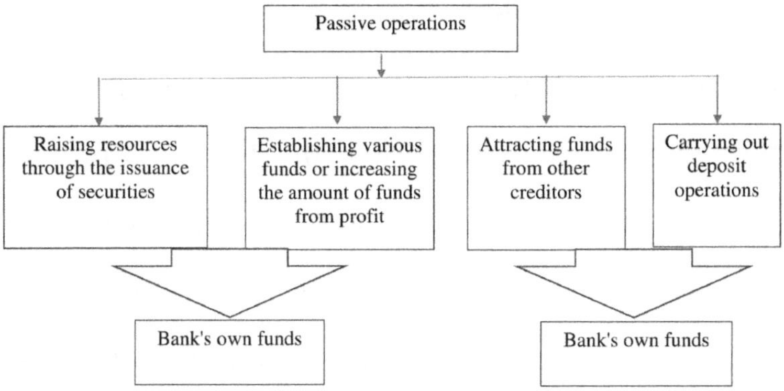

The above scheme shows that as a result of the first and second operations, the bank's own funds arise, while the last two operations generate attracted resources for the bank. The composition of the bank's own funds includes:

1. The bank's authorized capital;
2. The bank's reserve capital;
3. Special funds;
4. Material incentive fund;
5. The bank's retained earnings;
6. Various other established funds.

In practice, 20% of banks' liabilities correspond to their own funds. Attracted funds constitute the main part of the commercial banks' credit resources. Attracted resources are sometimes divided into two categories: the first is attracted deposits, and the second includes other liabilities and purchased resources. These resources are used in carrying out the bank's active operations, meaning that the bank's resources are allocated to various sectors for the purpose of generating income. Since the passive and active operations of banks are closely interconnected, the composition and nature of the liabilities are reflected in the implementation of banks' active operations.

Commercial banks hold an integral role in the market economy through their position and activities. If we pay attention to the current activities of commercial banks, nearly all entities of the national economy use banking services. The active operations of banks are considered the defining part of their operations. The structure of assets refers to the ratio of various types of materials in the bank's asset balance. The quality of bank assets is determined by the asset structure, diversification of active operations, the volume of risky assets, critical and incomplete assets, as well as the volatility of assets.

Commercial bank assets are divided into four categories:

1. Cash on hand and cash equivalents;
2. Investments in securities;
3. Loans (ssudas);
4. Buildings and equipment.

If we group the asset composition by the main types of banking activities, the following conclusions can be drawn:

- Credit operations occupy the primary place in bank active operations, with their share ranging from 19.90% to 83.25%.
- Investments in securities take the second place (from 2.15% to 29.18%).
- Cash assets come third (from 0.2% to

12.94%).

- Other assets, depending on their accounting characteristics, cover a very broad spectrum in bank operations (from 2% to 78%).

Another important type of bank active operation is loans secured by goods, i.e., loans granted against pledged goods. For loans secured by goods, the bank provides the loan not at the full market value of the goods, but rather a part of it, usually not exceeding 50-60%.

Structure of bank active operations

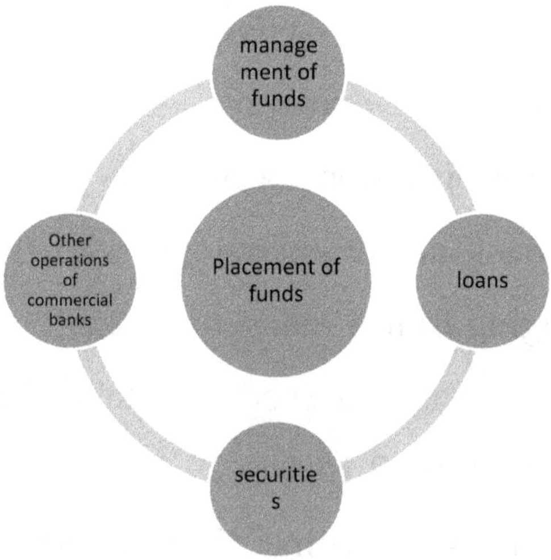

Loans: loans to other banks, loans to clients, investments in fixed capital.
Securities: investments in fixed capital and operations in the stock market.
Other operations of commercial banks: leasing operations, factoring operations, mortgage operations.

Another type of active operations of commercial banks is securities operations. Various securities are the objects of these operations.

From an economic perspective, asset management issues are considered separately from liabilities, but in practice, they are interconnected. It is difficult to carry out active operations without analyzing the sources of attracted funds in the liabilities section of the bank's balance sheet. The main active operations of commercial banks are lending activities.

During their activities, commercial banks earn

income from the services they provide. This income can take the form of fees, commissions, and transfers.

In recent years, leasing operations related to financing have significantly improved in commercial banks' activities. To explain this operation: banks lease machinery, equipment, and vehicles to industrial enterprises for long periods and enter into leasing contracts with them.

In this case, the bank purchases the equipment on behalf of the borrower and leases it to the consumers while retaining ownership rights. Here, the bank receives leasing payments (rent) instead of loan interest. For enterprises, leasing is one of the special methods of financing investments.

Leasing operations involve three parties: the lessor, the lessee, and the supplier.

The **lessor** is a specialized financial enterprise that performs financial functions.

Leasing, primarily being a means of financial investments and requiring reliable financial resources, is supervised by banks or their subsidiaries in global practice.

The **lessee** is a manufacturing or trading enterprise that leases equipment for use in the production process.

The **supplier** is the enterprise or organization that produces the object of the leasing contract; it can be a manufacturing or trading enterprise. Usually, the supplier and the lessee develop the main terms of the commercial contract. At the same time, the lessor (bank) reviews the financing conditions and signs the leasing agreement with the lessee.

Another type of financial operation of commercial banks is **factoring operations**. These operations are related to the circulation of payments on a wide economic scale. Factoring (from English "factor" – intermediary) is one of the new types of services in organizing settlements and coordinates the crediting of the client's working capital.

Within the active operations of commercial banks, the **lending process** occupies a central position. It includes the following stages:

1. Reviewing the client's application for obtaining a loan;
2. The bank assesses the borrower's creditworthiness and ability to repay;
3. The decision of the credit committee;
4. Formalizing the credit agreement;
5. Disbursement of the loan;
6. Monitoring the repayment of the loan and interest by the bank.

All loans issued by commercial banks are reflected in their loan portfolio. According to foreign economic sources, "Bank loans serve to cover expenses aimed at fundamentally renewing production, expanding it, producing new goods, and improving quality by attracting new technologies in the process of economic growth."

The credit portfolio of commercial banks can be classified based on the sources of financing and the regional position and location of the borrower.

Currently, centralized loans are issued in national currency according to government decisions aimed at developing priority sectors. Refinancing loans and loans provided from the bank's own funds can be issued either in national currency or in foreign currency when the client is creditworthy.

Among the operations of commercial banks, lending occupies a primary position. Loans granted by commercial banks are one of the key operations in banking activities. According to the Law of the Republic of Uzbekistan "On Banks and Banking Activity," the definition of a bank includes the requirement that it must carry out three operations, one of which is lending. Although the global banking practice understands the term "bank" as a financial department store, lending operations still hold a significant place in the activities of all banks.

On one hand, bank credit is an important resource that helps economic entities resolve temporary financial difficulties when necessary. On the other hand, it is the most profitable operation among those conducted by banks.

Banks, as specialized credit institutions, implement their credit policies taking into account economic and political conditions, the level of development of banking legislation, interbank competition, and the development level of banking infrastructure.

In order to attract the population’s idle funds, in 2015 the National Bank for Foreign Economic Activity of the Republic of Uzbekistan offered seven new term deposit products in the national currency to the public. Notably, these included the "E'zoz" term deposit dedicated to the state program "Year of Honoring the Elderly," the "Istiqlol" deposit dedicated to the 24th anniversary of the Republic, and the "Matonat" term deposit launched in connection with the Day of Remembrance and Honor.

As of January 1, 2016, there were 11 types of deposits available to individuals within the National Bank system, of which 22 were in the national currency and 8 in foreign currencies.

For senior clients, the National Bank offers the "Pensionniy" term deposit. For children under 16 years old, savings deposits such as "Nihol" and "Boychechak" were opened in both national and foreign currencies.

As a result of the Bank's efforts, the balances on the population's deposit accounts increased by 20% compared to the previous year, reaching over 1 trillion soms as of January 1,

2016.

Additionally, for more than 20 years, the National Bank has maintained a leading position in issuing and servicing plastic cards. To date, the National Bank has issued approximately 2.5 million plastic cards, including 1 million cards operating on the new online system and 112 thousand international Visa cards. The fulfillment of tasks set by the Bank's management and the Central Bank has contributed to an increase in the number of clients who prefer O'zmilliybank plastic cards as a cashless retail payment instrument.

To maintain a high level of service for plastic cardholders, the National Bank places special emphasis on expanding and continuously updating the service infrastructure. As of January 1 of the current year, the Bank had installed more than 20,300 payment terminals, through which transactions worth over 3.4 trillion soms were conducted in trade and service enterprises during the past year. The majority of people prefer to conduct payments in a cashless form using plastic cards rather than cash.

The balances on accounts opened under the national currency plastic cards amounted to 280.9 billion soms as of January 1, 2016, while for Visa international cards, the balance was 15.5 million US dollars.

The turnover at trade and service enterprises for Visa international cards reached 42.8 million US dollars. The number of ATMs servicing these cards was 11, and the number of POS terminals was 120.

Since 1993, the National Bank, a key member of the Visa international payment system, also gained the same status in the MasterCard international payment system on January 21, 2016. In the near future, local trade and service enterprises will have the opportunity to sell their products online not only using Visa cards but also MasterCard cards.

Currently, the Bank is working on creating an infrastructure to support contactless card services. This year, it is planned to launch a project to serve Visa and MasterCard international contactless cards through POS terminals. The project is scheduled to be implemented in June 2016, ahead of the meeting of the heads of member states of the Shanghai Cooperation Organization (SCO) held in Uzbekistan.

Additionally, to provide clients with important information about their remote transactions and allow them to monitor their accounts, the Bank offers information services such as SMS notifications, personal web cabinets, and IVR services to clients with local and international cards. Approximately 247,500 clients are currently using these information and service options.

In summary, commercial banks are the "circulatory system" of the economy, providing necessary financial resources to the economy by distributing the accumulated savings of the population and businesses. This intermediation acts as a factor that supplies the "fuel" required for further economic development. Thus, the operations carried out by banks include accepting money into current or other accounts, providing loans with or without interest, executing exchange orders, buying securities and shares, fulfilling clients' orders, granting loans secured by goods or goods documents, as well as other paid and cashless settlement operations.

References:

1. https://nbu.uz/uz/news/milliy-bank-yana-bir-marotaba-aholi-omonatlarini-jalb-etish-bo-yicha-yilning-eng-yaxshi-banki-bo-ldi/

2. https://lex.uz/acts/-1464935
3. A.A. Omonov, T.M. Qoraliyev. *Money, Credit, and Banks*. Textbook. Tashkent, “Iqtisod-Moliya”, 2012.
4. I.R. Toymuhamedov, R.R. Tojiyev, A.A. Azlarova, N.R. Bazarova, N.G`. Sattarova. *Money and Banks*. Textbook. Tashkent, 2021.

TABLE OF CONTENTS

Norqulova Shahzoda was born on April 27, 2005, in Surxondaryo region. She is currently a student at the Department of Finance and Financial Technologies of Termez State University. She is a holder of a university scholarship. Additionally, she has actively participated in many events and has earned achievements.

This book is a collection of more than 10 articles written by Norqulova Shahzoda, where readers can obtain essential information on certain topics.

I have published many scientific and research works, including the popular scientific treatise "The World Financial and Economic Crisis: Its Essence, Causes and Impact", the textbooks "Fundamentals of Taxation", "Taxes and Taxation", and the textbook "Accounting and Audit". More than 60 of my scientific articles and theses have been published in the collections of prestigious international and republican conferences.

I improved my skills by participating in scientific seminars in a number of foreign countries. From June 27 to July 5, 2015, I participated in a seminar on "Agricultural Management in Uzbekistan" in the town of Triesdorf, Germany, on the basis of a grant from the TEMPUS project implemented within the framework of the Erasmus+ program of the European Union. rom 2007 to 2013, I was a teacher at the Department of Finance of Termez State University, and a senior lecturer at the Treasury Training Center under the Ministry of Finance of the Republic of Uzbekistan. From 2013 to 2014, I was a senior lecturer at the Department of Finance. From 2015 to 2017, I was a senior lecturer at the Department of Economics. I was also the official representative of the Information and Search System "Norma-Hamkor" LLC in the Surkhandarya region. From 2018 to 2021, I was a senior lecturer at the Department of Finance and Deputy Dean for Academic Affairs of the Faculty of Economics and Tourism. From 2021 to 2022, I was the Head of the Department of Finance. From 2023 to the present, I have been working as an associate professor at the Department of Finance.

www.ingramcontent.com/pod-product-compliance
Lightning Source LLC
Chambersburg PA
CBHW070644240926
51846CB00003BA/775
* 9 7 8 9 3 6 9 0 8 6 2 7 6 *